THIS BOOK
belongs to

_____

Every day and every night the Sun watched the order in the Solar System.

Eight planets circled the Sun.
They were small and big, hot
and cold.

The Sun loved every planet.
It cared for them, warmed them
with its warm rays.

One day the Sun
started to count the planets.

Mercury

Venus

Earth

Jupiter

Saturn

Uranus

Neptune

Something was
wrong.

The Sun began to worry. Where was Mars? Where had he gone?

All the planets began helping the Sun. Again and again, they called out to Mars.

Suddenly, Neptune shouted:
"He's here! I have found him!"

Mars was hiding among the
many meteorites. He was very
sad.

The planets asked all at
once: "What has happened?
Why are you here?"

Mars quietly got out of his hiding place and started talking about his problem.

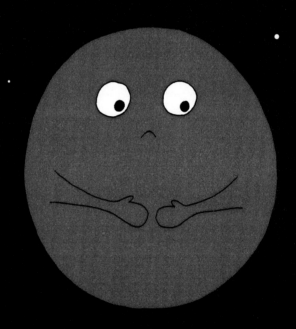

"It seems to me that I am the most ordinary. You are all so amazing, and I ... "

"What are you talking about?" the frustrated Sun asked. "Why do you think so?" the astonished planets asked.

Mars said: "Sun, you are a huge star. Your rays light everything around."

"Mercury, you are so interesting. You have one side that is hot and the other is cold."

"Venus, you are a bright planet. Who else can boast of her own shadow?"

"Earth, you are a beautiful planet. Your seas, oceans, forests, and mountains amaze me."

"Jupiter, you are a real giant. There is no one bigger than you."

"Saturn, you have rings that consist of millions of small stones."

"Neptune, you are the coldest planet. Even your gas turns into ice."

"And now look at me. There is nothing interesting in me. I'm not worthy to be a part of the Solar System".

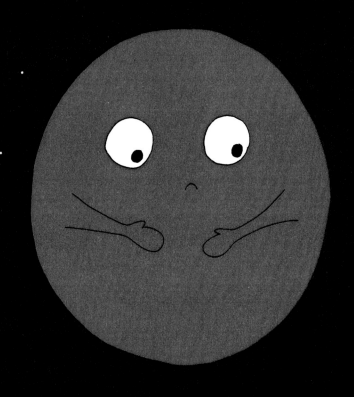

The Sun and the planets looked at each other and smiled.

"And how beautiful your canyon is! This is a real miracle!" exclaimed Venus, Saturn, and Uranus, to show support.

"I have many mountains, but even Mount Everest can not be compared to your mountains!" said the Earth.

"You see," said the Sun, "we are all different. You do not need to be like the rest."

"And we cannot imagine our Solar System without you."

Mars sighed with relief: "Thank you, my friends! What would I do without you? "

Since then, this space family has lived happily, because they appreciated each other.

THE END

Made in the USA
San Bernardino, CA
05 December 2018